AF478692

Bruce Russell

GMT

Glyphs, Morphs and Tropes

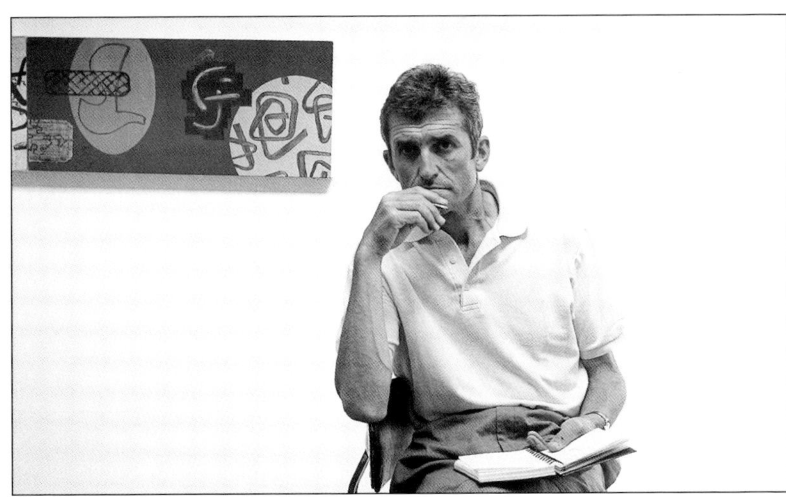

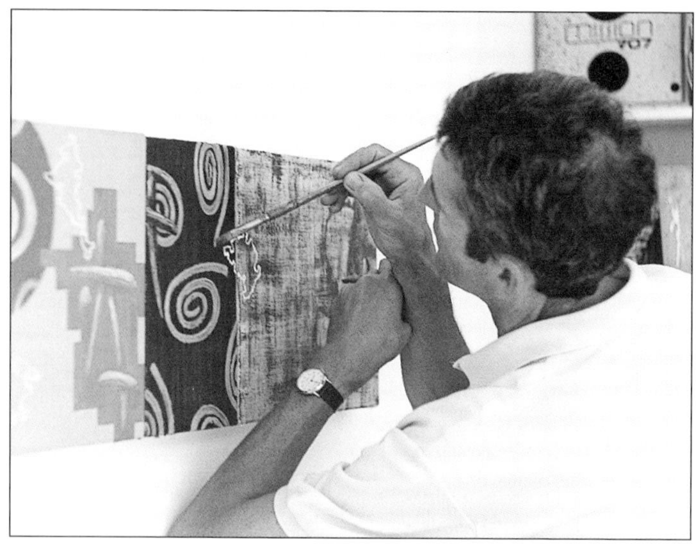

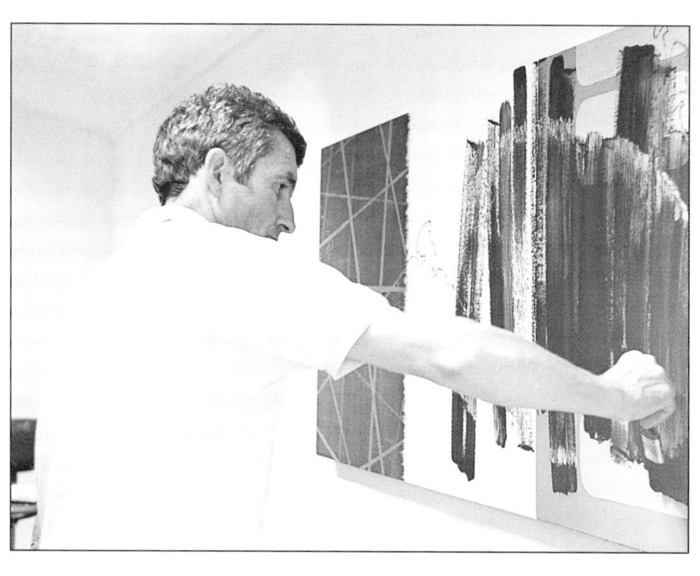

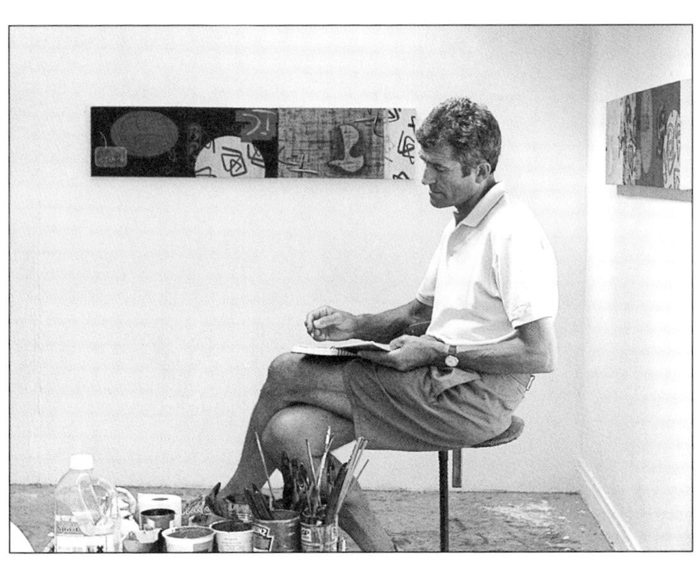

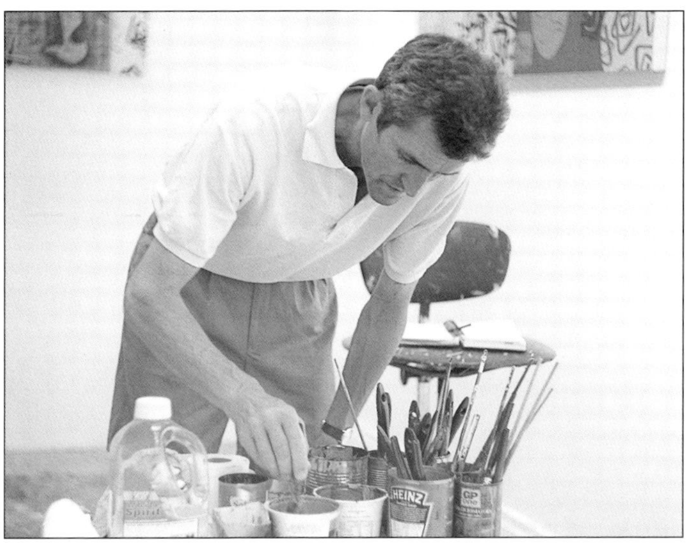

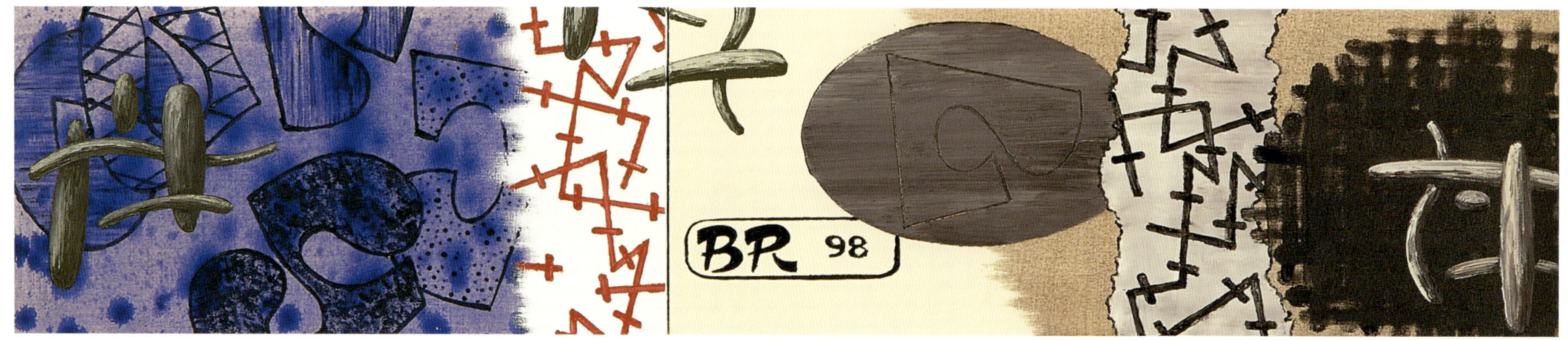

to Alison, Jack, Amelia, Rowena and Phyllida

Playing the Game When the Rules Have Been Changed: The Paintings of Bruce Russell

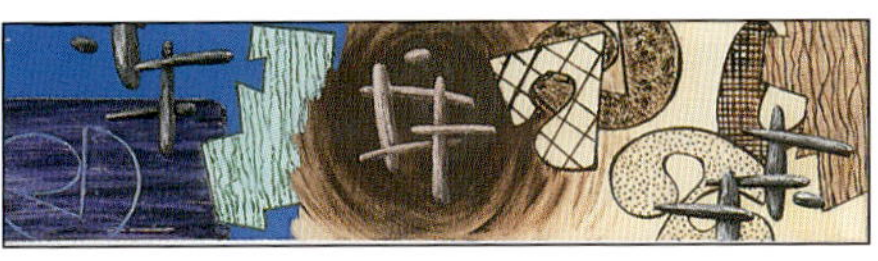

And of course, I have always loved games, with their etiquettes and procedures, their characteristic webs of space and time, their various sanctions of chance and order, and their frameworks conferring value or constraint; the parole of number, suit, touchline, goal and net. Games seem to be a comic attempt to provide an ordering metaphor for life's tragic absurdity, to give narrative or dramatic shape to inchoate flux.[1]

Anyone for postmodernism? Bruce Russell's series, *Glyphs, Morphs, Tropes*, teases out the playful strands of that controversial term. The symptoms of the postmodern 'condition', which having arguably now passed seem more connotative of a recently cured illness, are indeed thematically contemporaneous with the emergence of his painting. The mid-to-late 1970s witnessed the accretion of pomo's key features and references: the primacy of surface, language and image; the heterogeneity and fragmentation of consumer culture; the collapsing hierarchies of aesthetic value; Jean-Francois Lyotard's philosophical emphasis on gaming in the absence of metaphysical and aesthetic rules; and the intellectual pragmatism of Richard Rorty's enquiry into the immediate horizons of what is and what is not possible for philosophy. However, Russell's work does not spring from the postmodern per se as it is also constituted at a moment when such issues conflicted with modernity's various political, cultural and social claims to truth, reason and freedom. This transitional and turbulent period can be summed up by a key question: to what extent could rules (aesthetic, cognitive, ethical, political) be construed consensually rather than coercively? Who makes the rules, who should play by them and when must those rules be changed? Such grand questions seem far removed from this current body of work, but the latter is part of a genealogy which can be traced back to that period of cultural anxiety, and which can be identified as arising formally and discursively out of that conflict.

Since then, however, his painting has undergone marked transformation. In the 1970s, his employment of the trope of the game was drawn more from a visual than philosophical origin; his diamond-shaped *Gallowgate* series of 1977 was an eponymously imagistic synthesis of the structure of the Newcastle United FC stadium, in which the ground's brutalist modern stands and curvilinear corrugated roofing were reorganised under an abstractionist rubric. Lately, though, the 'game' has become an increasingly structural, quasi-systematic principle in his work, and much more than a metaphor. It is this trajectory that I want to trace, with reference to the other games played between competing factions of the art world in its turbulent

transition from modernity to postmodernity. I will
begin, however, with some rash generalisations which
should, I hope, adumbrate the key themes of the
game, rules and the conflictive dynamics of which all
games consist.

Painting as a Ludic Activity

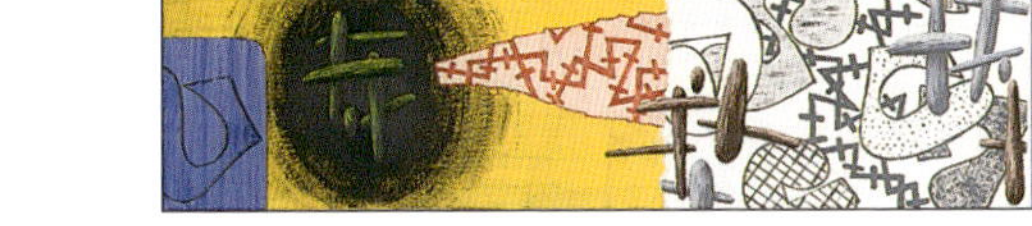

Painting, like most
modern art, imagines
itself as a ludic (playful) activity which, through its
participants, is thought to function in an autogenous
way (it generates itself, albeit with the assistance of
an artist) according to a set of rules, even when
those rules incorporate aleatory (chance-like)
processes. Furthermore, the history of painting can
be considered as one where, at certain moments and
places, rules were often imposed extrinsically (the
image having to subscribe to a moral, religious,
political and often didactic matrix) which could judge
paintings' individual or collective success or failure.
Certain 'rule-sets', such as those of the avant-garde,

ensured that the game played became an expression
of the rules made (as was the case with some
Cezanne, or Cubism, in which the parameters were
relatively evident in the facture). The painting game
can have more or less rigour, and varying degrees of
latitude, according to the conditions stipulated by the
rules, from Duchamp's conceptual ambiguities to
Greenberg's abstract formalism.

The Linguistic Turn

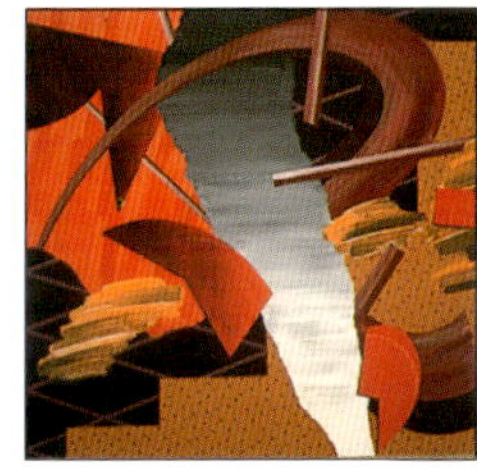

Russell embarked on his career
when the game of abstract painting
was problematic, when its rules
were open to contestation or
refusal, where some people no
longer wanted to play, and where (at the risk of my
straining the metaphor still further) the boundaries of
the game were transgressed or disrupted, as was
the case with the formalism's fear of kitsch, or
minimalism's aversion to the maximal.

The gaming metaphor for painting of the period
must be qualified by all external threats to the rules

of the game, as other games threatened to intrude. His painting carried high stakes in the 1970s as it emerged when art's rules had taken a 'linguistic turn', as incursions by theories of discourse and signification impacted on the visual culture in general. Such a paradigm did not fit well with the loosely affiliated group of London-based artists - Russell, Gary Wragg, Jennifer Durrant, William Henderson - whose work was considered to be lodged in a perceptual/formal rather than cognitive/linguistic framework, and not best equipped to articulate such structuralist and poststructuralist concerns.

Language could no longer remain a tool used simply for extracting the meaning from the painting using perceptual or 'close' criticism, and could not be restricted to the important task of revealing the image as an ideological product of historically specific socio-economic conditions. Language itself now became the object of language: the text was considered the locus of identity, image and object; those who misread Derrida even claimed that nothing lay outside that text.

Since the 1970s theory has extended itself beyond conflictive models of class and society to visual culture, where linguistic codes of film, advertising, television and art were thought to construct identity in ways irreducible to previous referents (such as class position). Thus, the primacy of the Word became the main issue for visual codes even if their codes were not primarily verbal or textual. Russell's painting was produced after the first phase of the linguistic turn, after the sorties of conceptual art, the ideology-critique of Art and Language or the coded precision of serial music. It was a time when theory, at its most strident, sought to erase boundaries and interrogate hierarchies; not only did it appear for many to assume the role of radical culture previously exemplified by the avant-garde of the 1960s, but its 'hypercriticism' also elicited hostility from some areas of the arts as a consequence.

HIs painting therefore sprang dialectically from the post-avant-garde period when, in the face of theory, aesthetic innovation and political radicalism were not necessarily synonymous; indeed, the most demanding art was seen to be redolent of elitism and institutionalised cultural practice (think of Andre's 'Bricks' in the Tate). Now that the avant-garde had been absorbed by the institutes, it was no longer even valid to place radical cultural practice against more traditional modes of art. This transformation brought urgency to the debates on the place of the work of art, its forms of address, the site of its display, the relevance of its audience to its effectiveness, its status as message and as social value. The attempts to sunder the conservative links between public, gallery and artist in the 1960s had failed, and many artists opted therefore to embed these concerns in the art itself by basing it on aesthetic theories and political ideologies that the gallery system could not digest. The public, as ever, was left similarly alienated, and became more so when community-oriented work displayed bland, sociological, photo-documentary characteristics.

In some quarters of the British art scene lines were drawn between formalists and socio-materialist camps which, in hindsight, seemed so intent on their mutual critique that the stormclouds of poststructuralist and deconstructive theory passed over Britain and towards the USA largely unnoticed. The pages of *Artscribe*, for example, which provided a space for the work of Russell and others (sometimes labelled 'anti-systematic painting', alongside work by Martin Ball and Trevor Sutton[2]) defined itself against earlier work of the conceptually based, ideologically oriented show *Art Now* or the high minimalism of painting and sculpture from earlier in the decade.

Artscribe's pages stand as a document of the resistance to what the journal saw as the deadening weight of concepts which either constrained painting to brands of philosophy (Greenberg's Kantianism, Rosenberg's existentialism and Fried's phenomenology), or reduced it to more or less vulgar Marxist notions of the importance of art in its social role and sociological interpretation.

Certainly, Russell's art practice arises at an historical moment when aesthetic and political positions were defended rather than deconstructed in the texts that artists and critics circulated through discussion groups and 'position' journals such as *Artscribe*. The work was seen not only as symptomatic or illustrative of such debates but as problematic in relation to them. Artists, critics, historians and 'theorists' (the new recruits) took sides across a broad battlefront where the key point of contestation was the communicative relation of artist, work, critic and audience (i.e. the question of who is legitimated to legislate for the meaning of the artist's work) rather than the poststructuralist conception of the artist or viewer being 'spoken' by discourse, the infinite interpretability of the image or text, and the deconstructive enterprise which dismantled the primacy of expression and the self-evident presence of the artist's gesture.

Paradigm Shifter

So the paintings were played out in a period when the rules of the painting game were neither simply in transition, nor just being contested; they were becoming decentred, as culture underwent the paradigm shift from (broadly speaking) the modern to the postmodern. Given the luxury of

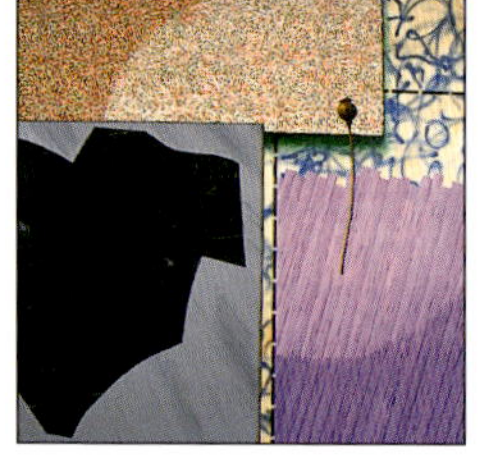

hindsight, it is possible to see how the formal and discursive position of Russell's work was therefore located at a historical point where a set of rules and games overlapped, and through which his work could be put into play in a number of ways, being seen as either symptomatic of: a flight from, or repression of, the socio-linguistic dimension of painting (the politics of representation, or the representation of politics that became a major concern of 1970s art practice and theory, as well as the analytical-philosophical dimension from Wittgenstein through to Conceptual Art); a compensational and Maximalist refusal of formalist art, object-art and the Minimalist culture of reductionism or reductivism (reducing complex symptoms to one cause, or reducing components to one essential form or idea); or a proto-postmodernist self-conscious abstractionism that took itself as a code in relation to other cultural codes, rather than as an integral, discrete and hermetic formalist practice. This latter interpretation is important, as it offers the possibility of registering Russell's art in its conscious use of references to mass culture and art history, and suggests that his work was fabricated less out of 'integrity' than integration in the face of the 'other' of culture now constituted as a set of differences (for example, in his incorporation of motifs extracted from the language of textiles design).

With Russell's painting, and at that time of epistemological crisis, you paid your theoretical money and took your interpretive choice.

Elitism and the Audience

Given this complexity the 'abstract' work of the late 1970s could, from one perspective or another, be judged as being either decadent or irrelevant. Against the earlier period of analytical, pared-down modernism his work could have looked like a step backwards, or a failure of nerve. However, that 'forward/backward' thinking was eschewed by contemporaries in his camp in order to open up criticism to other levels of response and in order to provide a 'richer vocabulary' for painting. Terence Maloon, for example, commented on the proscriptions placed on their work by formalist

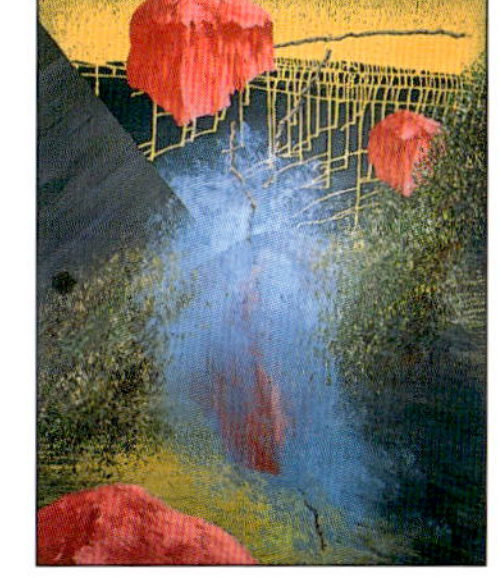

criticism, which contended that any dissimulation of the physical essence of painting could not be sanctioned, and that "transgressions were felt to be hopelessly *retardataire*."[3] This, however, could not sidestep the criteria demanded by those who claimed art should have a social, not to say socialist, responsibility.

A socio-materialist history of Russell's painting posed problems from the perspective of his intentions and those of his group because they did not produce work which had a didactic purpose or an investment in ideology-critique. The forging of links between society and art were not seen as directly relevant to them. However, it necessarily became the problematic for certain critics. In 1977, for example, Peter Fuller responded to his statement ("I'm an abstract painter and my first concern is with the formal integrity of the painting"[4] ; "the pure pursuit of pictorial quality"; Marxism has "compromised the integrity of the artists" by historicising art's transcendent, style-less values):
Russell's pursuit of the fiction of pure "pictorial quality", soon turns him into what he calls an "elitist", someone who regards himself as one of "a group of

individuals allied by a special commitment and subsequent attainment that transcends the workaday norm". Ah yes, pure painters, now almost a priestly caste, set apart from the mundane, base, material conditions of life, pursuing perfect formal integrity, and pure pictoral quality![5]

Fuller's criticism was launched from a platform that argued against the meaning of art being 'congealed' in the painting, and in favour of the constituting consciousness of the viewer of the painting who comes to it at a particular historical moment.

For Fuller such abstract, supposedly contentless formalism (he uses the term 'vacuous') which claimed universal, timeless validity was a highly specific, historically contingent form of painting. Its blindness to this fact meant that it could not transcend its time. It would, like the work of Cohen and Hoyland, and their "consumerist abstractions", merely attain the status of something historically worthy only of rejection by later artists.

James Faure Walker, painter, editor of *Artscribe*, and supporter of Russell, inveighed against such a historically-rooted perceptual model, stating that :

"if you are intent on seeing abstract paintings like they are meant to be signs, cultural traffic signs pointing the way to the future, then you'll miss most of what's going on. The meaning a formalist work does or doesn't have is located within the perceptual process and not outside of it."[6]

He stated that the mistaken conclusion to finding a work meaningful only when it appeared solely to be concerned about itself, was for the critic to think he has been duped by an aesthetic trick which concealed the painting's status as a mere commodity. For Faure Walker, the 'anti-formalist' lobby was incorrect because its target was hazily defined: it argued for historical and social accountability, or 'meaning'; however 'meaning' here took on the same mystical aura that formalists gave to 'quality'. He concluded that there was a critique of formalism going on in paintings such as those of Russell by dint of their allusive content and their complex vocabulary.[7] Like many artists who broke with high formalism yet remained within the abstractionist bracket, his work cannot be tidily registered along the axis of the dualism between formal integrity or social meaning.

In retrospect it could indeed be argued that, caught between the retreating flank of formalism, the conceptual/ideological cadres of *Art Now* and the dour Arts Council-funded community art supporters, this work could not very easily shrug off its supposed elitist and esoteric currency. Despite the claim that these artists themselves constituted a community, which stretched from Russell's studio in Shadwell[8], through Durrant's base in Peckham, to the Stockwell Depot studios, and which organised its cultural labour to include the task of criticism (*Artscribe* stems from here) in order to counter misinterpretation or miscomprehension, specifically by art journalists (the *Guardian* being the prime offender at that time), this could easily be interpreted as an elitist control of the works circulation and currency. Such perceived cultural elitism sat uncomfortably with much 1970s art production, which mainly consisted of an elaboration of collective, communal, localised, co-operative forms of production, display and reception. These were organised along lines which had only recently begun to be fully articulated, which meant that the class model, having formerly

constituted the framework of criticism, had at the time of its acceptance and relative gains already become mediated by issues of gender, race, sexuality, ecology and regionalism. This fragmentation of social formations doubtless transformed cultural production, but these new sites would further isolate the topology in which work such as Russell's was situated. As Faure Walker argued, in an attempt to offset accusations of elitism and ideological naivety, the assumption that the meaning of a work of art was determined by the context in which it is offered to the viewer was mistaken, as it concluded that if the context is objectionable, so too must be the art on display within it. He was referring in this instance to the *Hayward Annual*, and its selection procedures, as well as to the assumption that critics should always align themselves with the public rather than the 'highbrows'.

From the perspective of the late 1990s, one can see that this defence was perhaps a little simplistic; yet it has to be understood that the claim was made in resistance to the more obtuse notion that 'art should contact society' .

Indeed, Russell's then poorly received conviction that an elite was not a clique, but simply a group who were allied to a special commitment which transcended the everyday norm, found favour with the later YBA 'movement'. Artists such as Keith Coventry and Gary Hume would claim the status of a skilled group who strove for excellence, and for whom the idea of educating or reaching the public (or 'community') was a rather condescending one. They painted instead for a specific yet varied set of audiences, and their art was not reduced to a process of tapping into the consciousness of the proletariat.[9]

Additionally, while Faure Walker supported an intrinsic role for criticism (that artists should be able to take on the role of the critic) he and others of Russell's contemporaries shared with the later generation of young British artists a distrust of the mystificatory and theoretically deterministic theories that had arrived from the Continent. In Britain the excesses of poststructuralism and deconstruction had been the province of film theory, literary studies and art history; many painters and sculptors in Britain, however, were not so keen.

Theory - At a Stretch

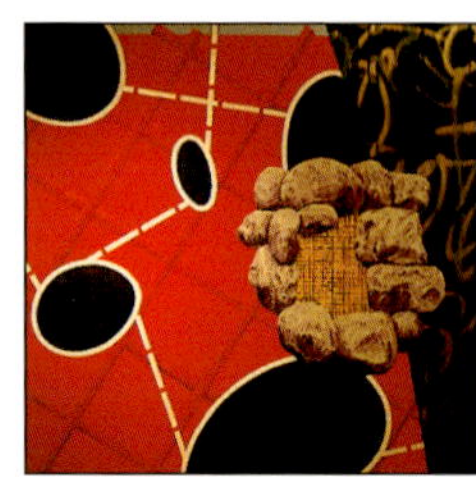

Russell's commitment to theory, therefore, was similar in one respect to those of the Artscribe editorials, in that he either rejected it or kept it at a healthy distance from the artwork in question. Interestingly, this tended to align him with those who, while being opposed to Russell's position in other respects, similarly thought such theory to be an hermetic activity.[10] With hindsight it is relevant to note that, when used, theories relatively new to the art world tended to provide ammunition for the continuing war-game between historicism and formalism. Fuller was on the side of history, but ambiguously so:

Put another way, this means the "essence" of painting cannot be said to reside within the material out of which the painting as object is made, but must be situated within the visual relationship which comes into being when those materials are seen.
Thus "pure painting" is not just a fiction. When posited as an intended (though unattainable) goal, it is a mutilation of a painting, a denial of that which is

essential to it. To borrow, for a moment, from the jargon of semiotics, the pure painter used his signifiers in such a way that they signify nothing except themselves.[11]

Fuller stealthily manipulated semiology, the science of signs, to illuminate the sign-function of 'formalist' paintings as images which referred only to themselves (paint as paint, colour as colour). He did so in order to deny this apparent hermeticism and to privilege the viewer, who brought an historical (future, present, past) perspective to the work.

However, Fuller's rhetoric in relation to works by, for instance, Russell, Cohen, Hopkins, Dellow and Hoyland simultaneously claimed that the images, while referring to themselves, barely existed as painting to anyone "outside the tight confines of the art world". Fuller was therefore attempting, paradoxically, to claim that a sign system existed which not only referred to itself (thus, logically, not accessible by anyone, including Russell), but at the same was capable of being accessed, not to say requisitioned, by a subject (Russell the 'elitist' who paints with self-referential language); yet was also a code that passed unrecognised by a public. This was certainly a very flexible version of semiology, (almost as if sign systems bestowed themselves upon, or withheld their favours from, the individuals they circulated amongst), and demonstrates its rhetorical and combative function at that time.

However, Fuller's wilful 'interpretation' certainly demonstrates not only that the linguistic turn had begun to intrude on British art, but that it had became clumsily superimposed as another rhetorical component in the battle between art factions of the time. Obviously, the conceptual movement had already set the mould for the incursion of language into art in the 1970s, articulated in the one case with Althusserian or Lacanian versions, whereby the work of Burgin, for example, assumed that language 'interpellated' the viewer and constructed the subject as a signifier in the symbolic order; and in the other case through its logical positivist and linguistic-philosophical aspects, which aligned conceptual art with the currency of the statement, performative utterance or language-game (Arnatt's "Keith Arnatt is an artist", or Joseph Kosuth's semantics of 'chair' or 'idea').

This is not to suggest, however, that theory was no-man's-land for Russell himself. Like many other artists and critics of the time, he certainly invested in the linguistic turn, although he did not adopt it as a methodological substrate to his work. In this respect his use of structuralist and poststructuralist theory was as selective as Fuller's; however, he did not employ it to such conflictive effect.

His eclecticism in this regard leads one to some improbable conclusions, the main one being that theory maintains a position in his oeuvre which, perversely, is as poststructuralist as theory can get: his project, while not extending to the linguistic, anthropological or semiological investigations of other artists, dovetails with his art's selective but pluralistic use of figural elements. He presents his theoretical borrowings as an inchoate, fragmentary and contradictory set of quotations, in contrast to the authorial, authoritative texts from which he draws. Such a 'writerly' response (here reproducing theory as literary bricolage) can be interpreted as constituting a text which is even more postmodern that the material from which it springs. For example, he writes:

Ferdinand de Saussure, the Godfather of twentieth-century structural analysis, contended - over eighty years ago - that "meaning is not the result of a correlation between the sign and a thing, but rather the product of a systematic play of differences among signs themselves". I warm to this, and to Rosalind Krauss' inference . . . "What is systemised in collage is not so much the forms of a set of studio paraphernalia, but the very system of form".

All this talk of system, structure and 'code' (for he also inserts Baudrillard) would, if one had not seen his painting in development from the 1970s to the late 1990s, give the impression that his painting was a rigorous investigation into the structuralist principles by which paintings could be organised or read in the earlier stages of the postmodern period. However, one may also see his employment of such terms as an example of the productive interpretation (similar to Fuller's) that painting adopted in its discursive conflicts at the time. Fuller had leapt to the conclusion that the severing of the sign from the world (signs now referring to each other within their own matrix) was a trick that formalism played to ensure it perpetuated the severance of the visual language of painting from historical contingency.[12] Russell, while not a formalist, wanted an enclosed system of meaning, which would bracket off formal values from the world. Both versions, of course, misread structuralism, which is based on the principle that meaning, being generated by relations between elements, cannot therefore be immanent to those elements (as quality, essence or integrity) or solely brought to them by the historically constructed viewer. In this manner, theories which demonstrated that painting was an effect of difference were commandeered and paradoxically enlisted to demonstrate essential truths about the image - either in relation to the constituting primacy of the historically-rooted individual (which structuralism in fact ignores), or in relation to enduring pictorial values. One can see, therefore, that semiology was messed around with in order to prop up the arguments of the so-called formalists and apparent historicists.

Fortunately, Russell's flirtation with structuralism and systems of knowledge and representation did (and does) not give them space to become the generative principle of the work; indeed, they are themselves simply references which (*contra* Fuller) merely reveal the choosiness of his enterprise not just at a visual but also a textual, theoretical and literary level. In short his use of theory is quotational rather than foundational. Indeed, given the weakening grip of textual theory on painting, it seems that he is aware that the writings of Krauss, Foucault, Baudrillard et al no longer threaten to supplant the work of painting, and can therefore be utilised illustratively without making their positions overwhelm the work.

So formalism and textualism both constitute elements in his game, but his painting cannot simply be reduced to either. Looking at *Glyphs, Morphs, Tropes*, at those patterns and forms which cascade or slide across and beneath the picture plane, the 'meaning' is neither hermetic and 'in itself', nor terminally referential or intertextual (as poststructuralism has it). Moreover, since the painting ensures that the two positions are conflated an ambivalence arises which serves to keep conceptual or perceptual 'closure' of the image in suspense. Before describing this dynamic I should bring out the referential dimension of his work to counter accusations of formalism (as if anyone uses such criticisms these days!).

The Taste Police

A fine example of Russell's referential gaming (or its interpretation as such) is evinced in a text by Matthew Collings who, on his first ever art assignment, slides into ersatz-critique for his 1979 review of the "new waver" Bruce Russell, whose "fab new paintings" are named after dances like the 'Jive' and 'Quickstep' and which are culturally charged to the point of tastelessness :

The new discoramas aren't likely to cause any controversies in the art world. Fans and initiates will revel in the sharpness and zippyness. The snappy, ying-yang structures and chic, interior decorating/expensive men's wear colours - burgundy reds and lime greens, khakis and coffees and burned oranges, pearly whites and navy blues. Everybody else will either ignore the show altogether or else sneer at all the blatant decorativeness and derivativeness and art historical in-jokes. Detractors will also deplore the vulgar eclecticism and opportunism and lack of any weighty "content".[13]

But Collings was surprised to find himself enjoying the work and its appealing colours: porridgy bars of Euston Road blacks, ochres and creams; wasteland grey and Fablon pink; greens like sunlight through a screen of rubber plants; and paintings reminiscent of BBC2 adaptations of novels by Somerset Maugham. His conclusion was that the longevity of the paintings became as uncertain as the *Gallowgate* series, which was already "beginning to look decidedly dreary." There was a danger, he warned, that the current dance series would either look boring, neat or just hopelessly dated.

Such criticism barely distinguishes the historical particularities of his painting from those of innumerable artists of the previous hundred years, whose painting of the 'now' were always destined to become an art historical 'then'[14], but it serves a purpose. Despite Collings' reluctance to push through the implications of the contradictions between the presumed attack on (or defence of) the innate and aesthetic permanence of quality in these pictures, and its decorative/consumerist subject matter (which in terms of theories of consumption must become stylistically obsolete in order to keep the wheels of mass production turning) there is an important conclusion to be made from such flippancy: Russell's morphological cultural references - the shapes, designs, colours from which he draws and which he mobilises - are part of an archaeology of sign systems which, being linked to design, fashion and style, must emit something of 'the dated' (to do so, indeed, is to rescue the paintings from ahistorical formalism). While it is not crucial to his endeavour to emphasise this dimension it should certainly be identified when critics attempt to construct his work as being in elitist opposition to a public. From the postmodern point of view, such work can be situated in direct relation to codes of mass consumption rather than the concerns of painting *per se*, as

subject matter about fashion cycles and obsolescence, and as a game which is played on the boundary points between the alleged authentic mark and the so-called inauthentic gesture.

This boundary was highlighted in Faure Walker's analysis of 1970s Pattern and Decorative Painting, particularly in shows such as New York's *Babylonian Oasis*, which displayed work that had also been recognised by Russell as departures from the strictures of formalism and the visual language games of conceptualism. Issues of style, surface effect, complexity, opulence, humour, paradox, disguise and the bizarre, discussed by Faure Walker and Russell, melded with the proto-postmodernist sensibility that Matthew Collings and others saw in Russell's work at the time. These themes persist in his paintings of the late 1990s.[15]

"At what points do these values conflict with those of 'pure' painting?" Faure Walker asked. What is the line drawn between a mark of integrity and a sham gesture? Does it make sense to speak of the formal integrity of the picture plane when its material is disguised by trompe l'oeil and shifts of cultural identity? These were questions that Russell was also attempting to answer, alongside those with whom he shared certain affinities: the off-stretcher work of Alan Shields, or the abstractions of Bill Conlon, Kim MacConnel and Katherine Porter. This interrogation, however, was not without risk. As David Sweet said: *With aggressive eclecticism the artists devour whatever content comes to hand and regurgitate it in a torrent of ciphers, imagery, personal motifs, art historical emblems, violent textures, crude tints and numerous bizarrely costumed pieces of vomit, through which float up new bastard shapes and mongrel symbols, the exotic progeny of some scandalous, if spirited, mass coupling of styles and periods. Which is fine, as far as it goes.*[16]

The problem for Sweet was one of producing painting that was sufficiently lithe and manoeuvrable to avoid flimsy associations with mass media and searing novelty on one hand, and falling into formal orthodoxy on the other. Successful painting would have to find a set of organisational principles which would make its eclectic elements coalesce. As can be seen from Russell's recent series, the rigour with which stylistic vocabulary has become registered in the pictorial structure within and between the paintings ensures that possible criticism on these grounds is rebuked from the outset. His work, however, is not merely a synthesis of chance and order, or style and structure.

From Structure to Deconstruction

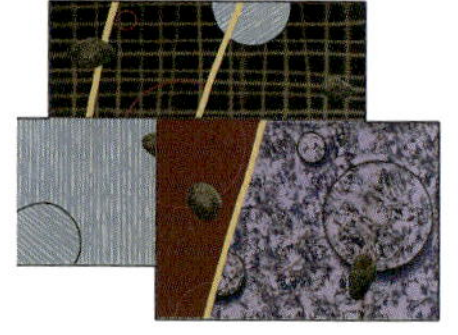

The series of work, *Glyphs, Morphs and Tropes*, shows how an increasing complexity of construction has brought the metaphor of the game into a more deconstructive setting than earlier works such as the *Gallowgate* series. It is one which features a collapse of hierarchies: between registers of the gesture and the mark, between the 'sham' and the 'authentic' and between the stencil and the hand. Whereas earlier paintings relied on masking tape, the architecture of the grid and the straight line to provide the rationale from which more gestural features could develop dialectically, the current work is far more able to collapse these dichotomies: curlicues, criss-crossed slabs of paint and initialled signatures trade on a type of painted mark which simultaneously connotes the hand-made, machine-printed and computer-generated. The paintings' intentionally troublesome hybridisation of the authentic, the sham and the simulated (they are no longer held apart, as each mark announces both its authority and its pretension) is derived as a consequence of Russell's realisation that the mark - the evidence of the hand - can be used to all these ends. These are brushmarks, in other words, which one can identify neither as postmodern distanciation (like Glen Brown) nor as modernist immediacy (such as de Kooning). The paintings threaten to render ambivalent the poles of the authentic and the false, yet prevent their involution in the ironic 'wink' of the postmodern. They are deconstructive rather that merely poststructuralist because deconstruction entails exposing how elements in a text spell danger, destabilisation and threat to the authority or 'truth' of that text (just as marks in a painting can be found to undermine the painting); poststructuralism, on the other hand, permits an endless, constantly deferred and often relativistic denial of authorial intention (which means that issues of intended quality or skill become redundant) in endless chains of signification. Poststructuralism, popularly understood, defines the pomo sensibility of total and constant instability, in which everything is susceptible to transformation into its other, and where the difference between essence and appearance is erased.

In this context, the formalism with which Russell was charged seems far removed from these current orchestrations of often misleadingly tremulous marks within such seemingly organised procedures. The skill lies precisely in collapsing the authentic/formalist/integral with the contingent/historicist/referential. On this account his project is one which insists that both utter doubt and complete certainty are lodged in the mind of the viewer: one is forced to think of his paintings as an attempt to find its essential quality in the marks themselves through reference to mass cultural sytems: the viewer is put in mind not just of the struggles over the integrity of the picture plane, but the wages paid to those factory artists of mass-produced landscapes and suchlike who reproduce the same symbols in the same place on countless paintings. While testifying to the consumerist logic of Russell's art, however, this is not to devalue the developed skills which allow for such readings; it simply draws attention to the productive articulation of the two fields of culture.

In this context, and if one is forced to return to those 1970s debates, his work always had a sense that its 'public' was identified with signs of mass consumption rather than with a specific class consciousness. If he is a formalist, his formalism draws from those forms which circulate in mass-manufactured culture and through which class was destined to be represented. His paintings operate, therefore, in partial difference from the formalist or retinal values that so many critics imagine form the credo of his work. This is because they incorporate a multitude of sign systems drawn historically from consumer, mass-public or more esoteric sign systems that he has encountered since childhood (1950s textile patterns, transport typography, aircraft design, Japanese prints of war scenes); however it simultaneously reinstates itself in its own carved-out presence as its formal structures organise sign-systems anew for the expediency of each painting, from one painting to the next. Russell's painting is, temporally, now and then.

However, the fact that his art was and is not reducible to navel-gazing formalism is not the issue, because the paintings provide as non-hierarchical an awareness of the Other (thus not simply referring only to its own integral characteristics) as more obvious, 'quotational' postmodern art. Moreover, the previously unfashionable but recently more acceptable clues which he leaves in his painting and (despite his distrust of discursive support) explains in his writings and discussions of his work, show how autobiography informs his production: his references to 1940s and 1950s Hollywood film credits, where a hand delicately turns a page, or in which sun shines through leaves in Southern States; industrial design and machinery; typefaces (he initially trained as a graphic designer); aeroplane and other transport design; cutaway diagrams, rock 'n roll record covers; architectural blueprints; de Kooning's metropolitan slant in *Excavations*[17]; *Stella's Aluminium Painting*[18]; the work of his tutor, Jeremy Moon, whose triangular wedges arrowed into one another, shifting from ordered to random pattern; and the phased modes and figures of minimalist music, particularly the work of Steve Reich - all these references are present in the narrative typologies of his art.

Glyphs, Morphs and Tropes

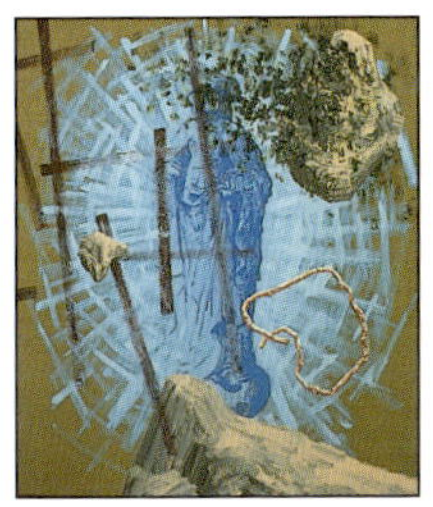

Since the show of his *Dance* paintings at the Hayward in 1979, and the Schnabel-like figurative elements of paintings such as *Ailsa* in 1985, the intrinsic relations of the colours and forms of Russell's current paintings, as well as those between the paintings, have begun to simulate systematised procedures. For example, a 'key', identifiable in sections of the paintings that are painted in monochrome, is exploited in order to refer to the coloured forms mobilised across the picture plane. Careful viewing draws out the binarisms between this key and its referent, analagous to a map and a territory, a menu and a meal, a signifier and signified.

Further scrutiny reveals the use of wipes, fades and jump-cuts within, between and across the canvases as elements which are organised much like a movie or musical score. Often his work on a painting in the series compels him to return to a previous one, in order to reconfigure, redirect or reorchestrate the 'characters' that he has assembled as a family group or set. The work is not systematic *per se* because the composition is not generated by impersonal or automatic means. Rather, it is, as he says, more akin to a game, where a degree of risk, intuition and skill is afforded. Playing such a game carries him far from the structuralist or systematised conceptions of his work, and well beyond formalism. Even when conceived as a series of codes with a solution, this is not to say that the paintings can brought under a linguistic and conceptual equivalent (that is what the aesthetic theorist Theodor Adorno called 'identity thinking'). As he insistently demonstrates, there is not a concept (ideological or linguistic) in which a painting can be adequately fitted. The rules of the game, in painting, differ from rules of other games, and they cannot be entirely tabulated in a rule book.

Endgame: 'Only what does not fit into this world is true' [19]

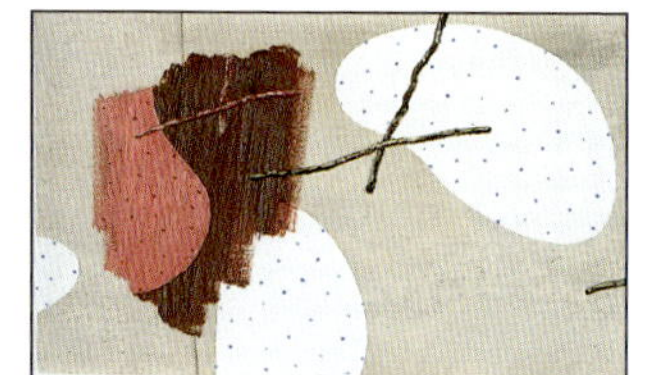

For Russell's generation the threat of making painting identical with (or understandable by) another system was instanced by the rationalising tendencies of linguistics and social theory. Such 'identity thinking' argued that for a painting to be 'true' it must be capable of being brought into the realm of concepts (such as those of the criticism of formalism, socio-materialism, linguistic theory). This thought is anathema to him and his contemporaries for it regiments the Other of the work according to frameworks which reduce it to variations of the Same. This represses the possibility of the non-identical: the sensuous and technical individuality of any particular painting, even when part of a series.

Simultaneously, while the art refers to mass culture in ways mentioned above, the principle of non-identity means that it cannot be entirely subsumed by the systematic rationality of mass culture. Russell's techniques and methods of ordering the 'residues' of other forms (the 1950s patterns, the typefaces, the maps) now stripped of their authority or discursive claims to truth, are brought under the principle of the non-identical: his glyphs, morphs and tropes insist that the elements and materials from which they hail are susceptible to another sort of integration, in a non-conceptual form of unification. Yet all the while his painting is an art which exists through its desire to be non-art, in its dreams of the series, the rule-bound, the rational, the linguistic and the conceptual. This is a game that cannot be won, but these tensions ensure that the game can at least proceed. While games are, as Bruce Russell said above, "comic attempts to provide an ordering metaphor for life's tragic absurdity", they therefore also desire to imagine that life is orderly, and that art can become identical with the latter's concepts (or rules). This is what allows art to be a game apart, buoyed up by its impossible dream of being brought under an integrating thought. This desire of art to be non-art - to be a key to the concept - is also, as Adorno says, the unhappiness which drives it forward. Games aren't always fun to play, which is the reason why they are so compulsive to the player.

Chris Horrocks, Summer 1999

Bibliography

1   Bruce Russell, '"Passion for the Code": An artist's confessions', Kingston University MS (1993)

2   Peter Rippon, 'Notes on New Abstract Painting', Artscribe No.10, Jan (1978):32

3   Terence Maloon, A Recent Tendency, Hayward Annual 1979, London: Arts Council of Great Britain, (1979):63

4   Note that Russell prioritises the formal concern but does not make it exclusive.

5   Peter Fuller,'Peter Fuller responds to 'Painting Now'', Artscribe No.6, April (1977): 32

6   James Faure Walker, 'James Faure Walker replies', Artscribe No.6, April (1977):36

7   James Faure Walker, 'Fertile Forms', Artscribe No16, Feb (1979):21 Walker's comments are interesting on

    account of their connection with recent literary theory . He was in effect opening up a path to the

    deconstruction of the term 'meaning' as it is employed by art-critical discourses.

8   Russell painted in studios adapted from housing originally constructed for labourers on Brunel's projects.

    Russell rented his space for £6.50 p.w. in 1976-77.

9   This does not discount the obvious simulations of proletarian art or the performative currency of working-class

    culture, which many artists adopted from the late 1980s onwards.

10 For example,certain feminist positions of the 1970s claimed that such theoretical mystifications did not serve

    the cause of women in everyday life.

11 Peter Fuller, (1977):33

12 Russell also draws on Michel Foucault's study of Velazquez' Las Meninas, which exemplifies the classical form of

    representation in which signs refer to each other under the authority of the absent subject (the king).

13 Matthew Collings,'Bruce Russell at Ian Birksted', Artscribe No.18, July (1979):57

14 This assumption also shows how in the late 1970s Collings had begun to intuit an historical moment that

    witnessed the collapse of the modernist search for the perpetually new into the consumerist logic of the

    fashionable, in a generalised circulation of sign-exchange values.

15 James Faure Walker, 'Babylonian Oasis,New York Commentary', Artscribe No.22, April (1980):16

16 David Sweet, 'Progress in an Era of Orthodoxy', Artscribe No.14, Oct (1978):43

17 Russell describes it as 'one more city painting - so different from the Stella, but for me equally exciting, this

    time because of its balance of drawing and painterliness, of visceral churning rhythms gated by a half-revealed

    angular grid'.(1998)

18 He calls Stella's work 'an urban painting where influences teem under its metallic surface - the grids of

    expressways, skyscrapers and parking lots, the hard sell and aluminium facade of the post-war American

    consumer dream - and conversely a kind of visual logical positivism, linguistically self-referential, resisting

    epistemological indulgencies'.(1998)

19 Theodor Adorno, Aesthetic Theory, trans. C. Lenhardt, London: Routledge and Kegan Paul, 1984:86

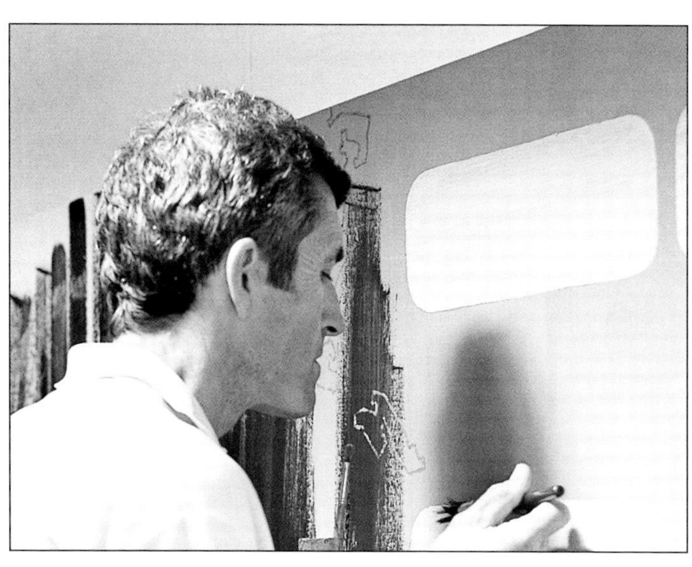
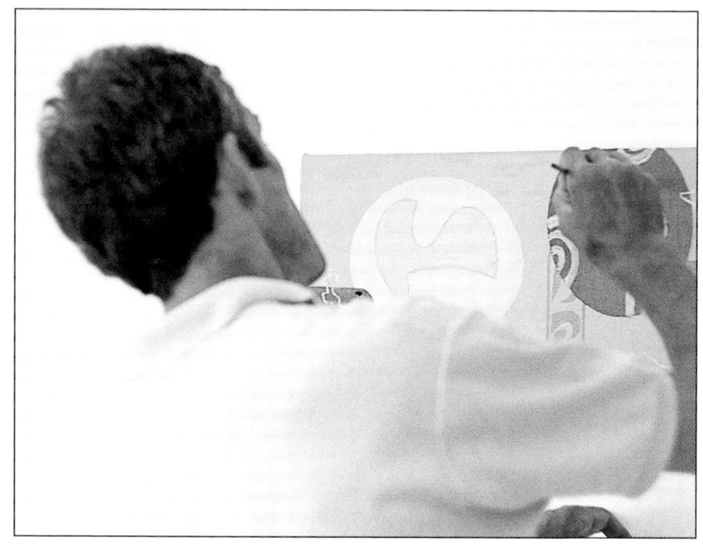

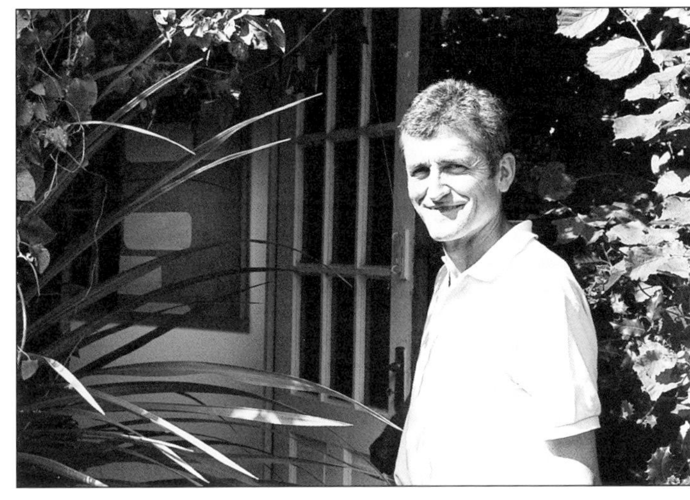

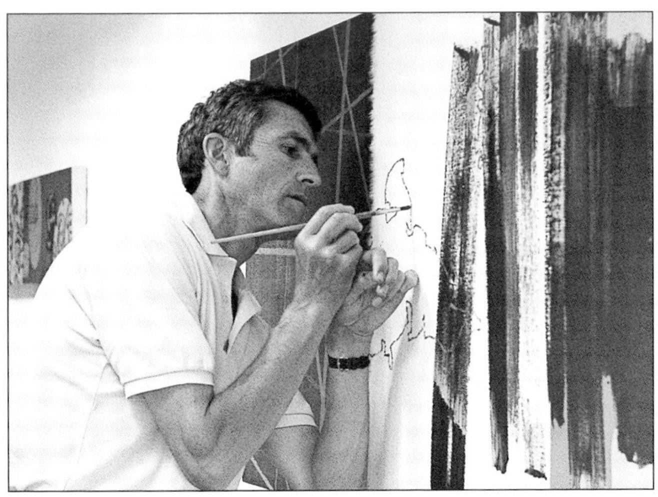

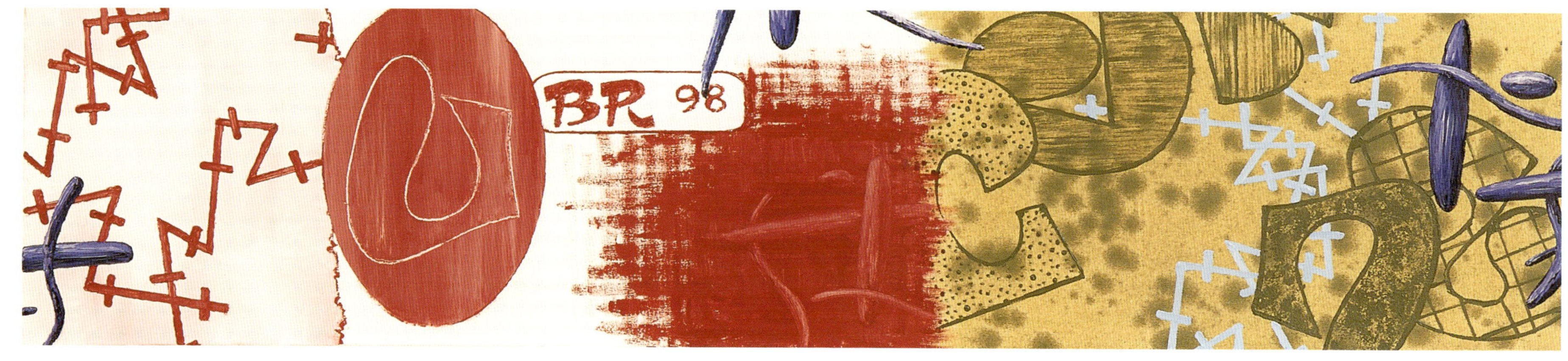

BR 98

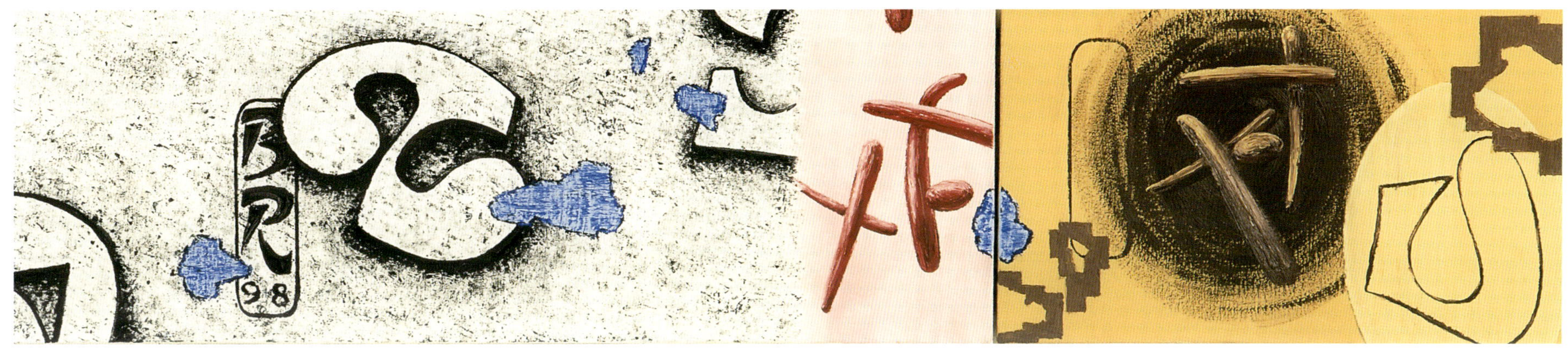

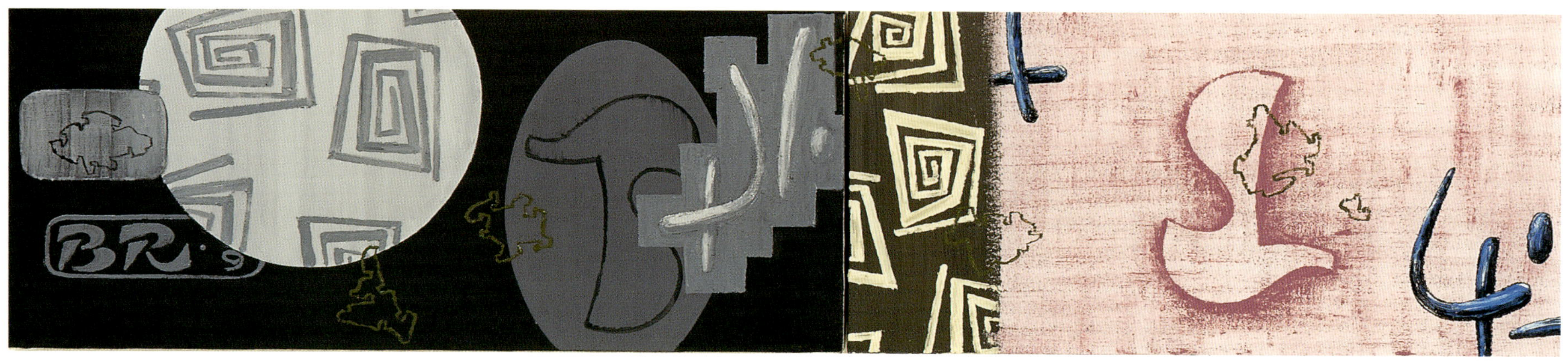

BR.9

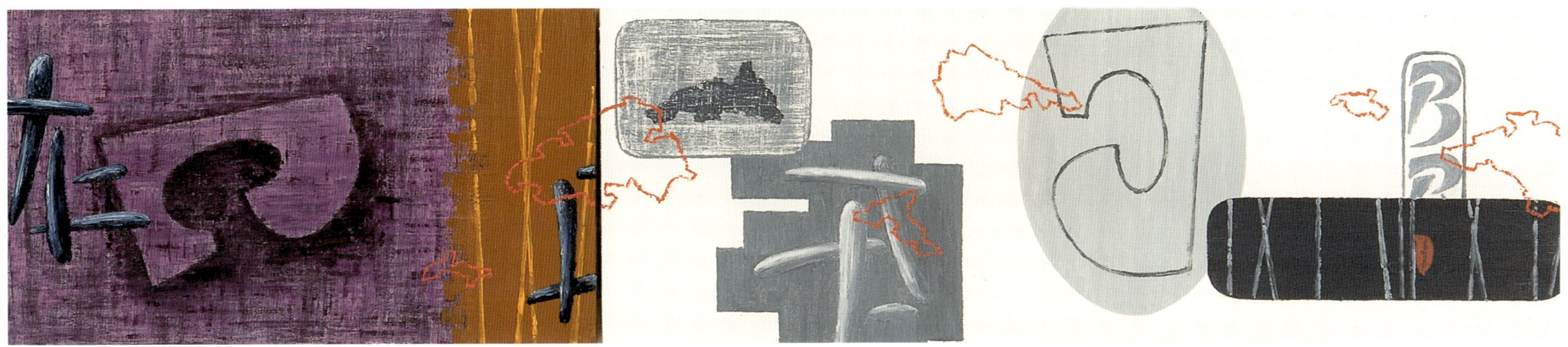

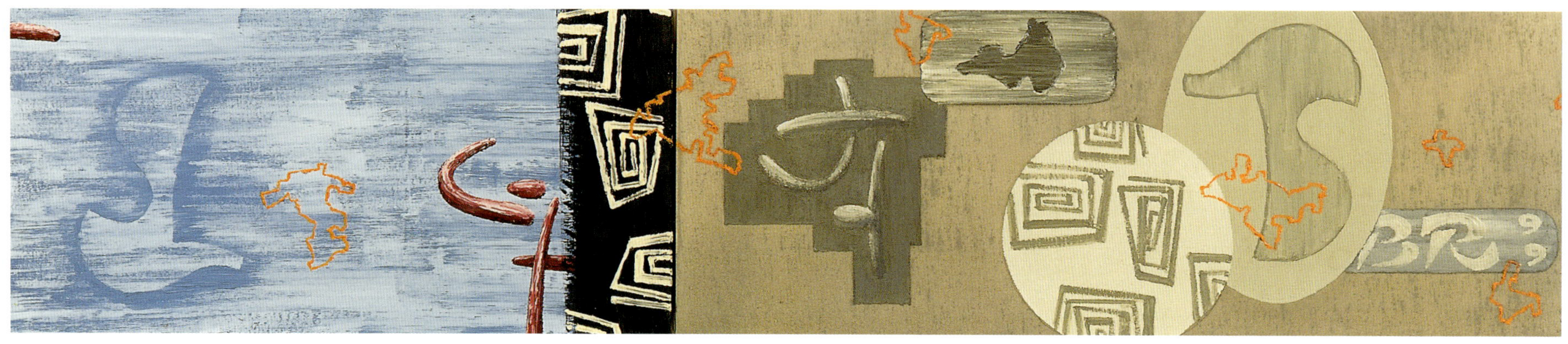

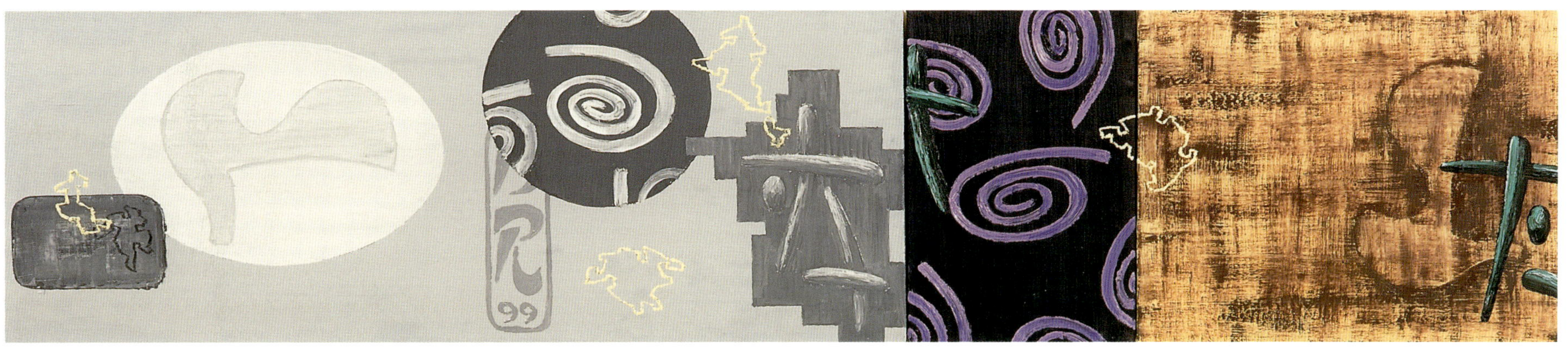

99

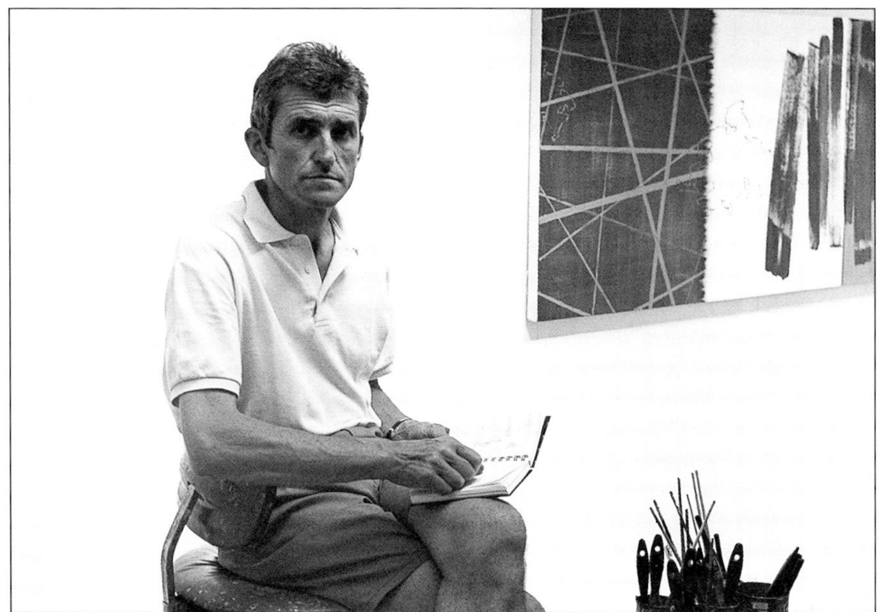

I've been painting seriously for thirty odd years, and it doesn't get any easier – I don't suppose it would be much fun if it did. That means that I've spent the equivalent of many months, possibly a year or two, sequestered in various studios. My first and most fervent thanks must therefore go to my wife Alison who has put up with this for a great portion of that period, and latterly my children, who know with unerring accuracy when not to cross the sacred threshold; thank you family, for your patience, indulgence, and great support.

As this catalogue and show seem to represent a kind of milepost in my career, I should mention other serious debts of gratitude. They go to those colleagues, friends and fellow artists, critics and gallerists who have taught me (or tried to), inspired me and encouraged me through friendship. It would be invidious to mention names from such a rich and varied crop, but I will anyway; those not mentioned are certainly not forgotten

Alan Gwilt, my first teacher. He convinced me I could be a professional artist, and steered me to Chelsea. A charismatic, inspiring man, who shaped my life.

John Hoyland, the biggest personality I've ever met, who showed me what ambition could achieve, and whose unforgettable 1967 Whitechapel show gave me a life's benchmark.

Jeremy Moon, who died tragically young and has left an irreparable hole in British Abstract painting. He was idiosyncratic, fiercely logical and did things with shape, sequence and order that made my spine tingle. He was a challenging teacher.

Bernard Cohen, who taught me self-discipline and an enquiring attitude. His forays between maximal and minimal, and his painterly handwriting that reveals an omnivorous knowledge of different cultures, leave an indelible mark.

Brian Young, evergreen maverick guru, who conitues to cut the crap from your brain and the scales from your eyes.

Tom Bromly, probably the most influential art educator of the last thirty years. He took a bet on me when I was very wet behind the ears, and he did the same for many others, who now run some of the best Fine Art schools up and down the country.

John Edwards, painter turned sculptor, and a great, no-nonsense teacher. He has a phenomenal eye for talent – in students and young teachers. He gave me another big break – into St Martins, and some memorable years in the middle of where it was all happening.

Albert Herbert, for his amused indulgence of my excesses – his impish laughter disguised a really serious artist/teacher; his effect was profound at St Martins.

More thanks for their friendship and professional example go to: Bill Henderson, Gary Wragg, Jim Faure-Walker, Jenny Durrant, Mick Bennett, Alex Ramsay, Tricia Gillman, Jim Latter, Michael Ginsborg, Prunella Clough, Martin Pace, Tim Allen, Derrick Haughton, Barry Martin, Derek Dalton, Gilbert Ward, Tony Harrild, Hugh O'Donnell, Richard Kidd, Judy Bibby, Howard Rogers, Martin Ball, Clyde Hopkins, Ann Rees-Mogg, Tony Whishaw, Mick Moon, Noel Forster, Patrick Caulfield, Merlyn James, Fenella Crichton, Vera Russell, Moira Kelly, Monica Kinley, Nancy Balfour, Jeremy Lewison, Michèle Roberts, Paula Rego, Peter Doig, Anthony Hill, Malcolm Hughes, Stephen Foster, Les Buckingham, William Varley, Richard Demarco, Edwin Easydorchik, Terry Setch, Alan Bond, Ian Stephenson, Paul Huxley, David Royle, Tony Eyton, Brian Eno, Alan Rickman, John Russell-Taylor, Gillian and Neville Jason, Zuleika Dobson, Neville Boden, Denis Bowen, Peter Dick, Frank Bowling, Derek Southall, Oliver and Nyda Prenn, Mike Gibbs, Colin Bloxham, Terence Maloon, Peter Rippon, Mathew Collings, Bryan Robertson, Brian Fielding, Bert Irvin, Basil Beattie, Jose Mouga, Benjamin Rhodes, Ian Birksted, Sonia Birksted, Robin Page, Paul and Claire Risoe, Richard Warner, Colin Crumplin, all the staff of the School of Fine Art, plus Keith Grant, Trevor Thorne, and all my many friends across Kingston University

This project would not have been possible without the support of the Faculty of Design's research committee. Particular gratitude to Sue-Ann Lee and Harri Ap Rees, for long-term good faith.

Special thanks for their continuing championship must go to my dealers Brian and Amanda Beardsmore

My absolutely final credit goes to the small and very talented team that have helped me put this catalogue together. Chris Horrocks, whose essay combines exhaustive research with a refreshingly personal interpretation of my work (he's told me more about it than I ever knew…): Dave Wood, the designer, and Charles Ryder and Jackie Thomas, who help me run the beautiful Stanley Picker Gallery at Kingston University, Vince Wade and Pauline Amendt. They are a very talented bunch. Congratulations team!

Bruce Russell, Summer 1999

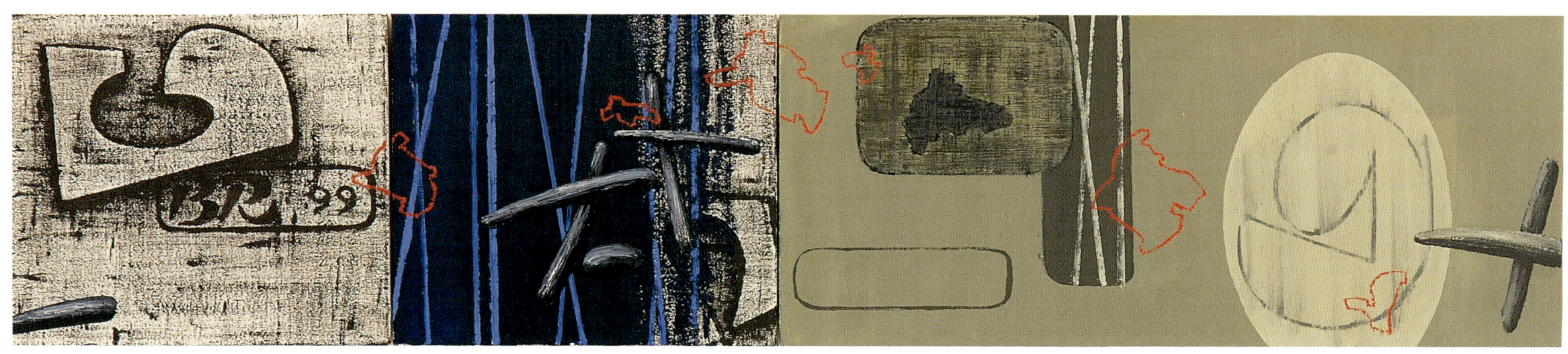

BR '99

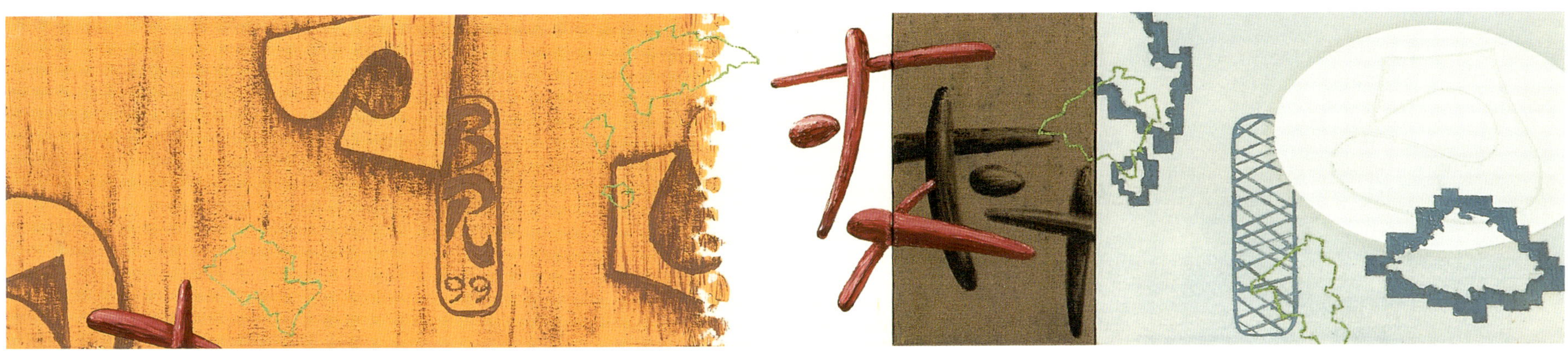

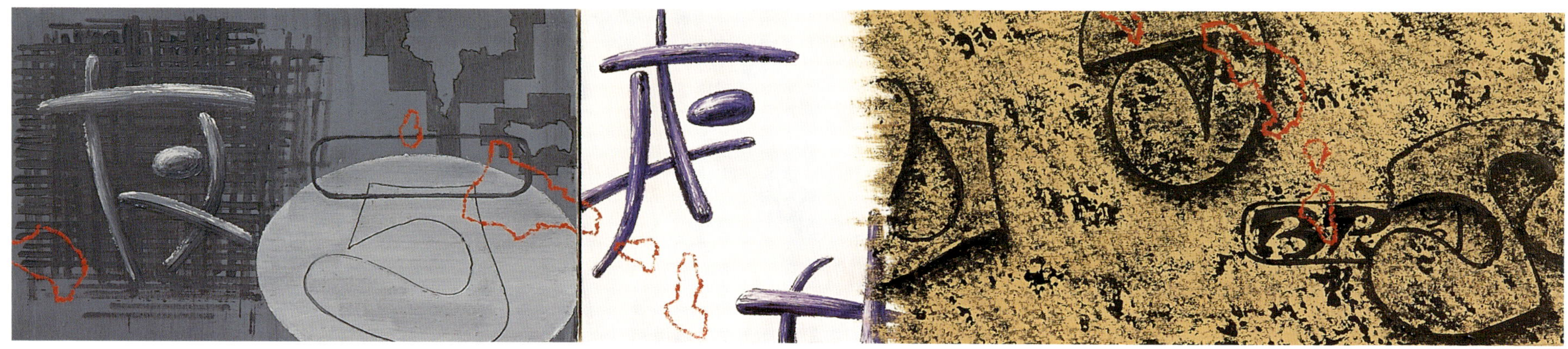

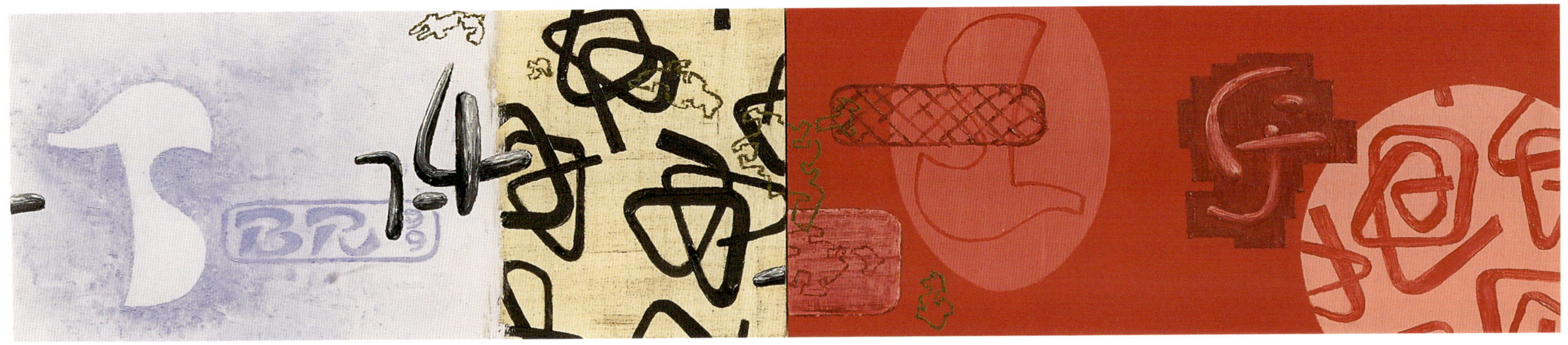

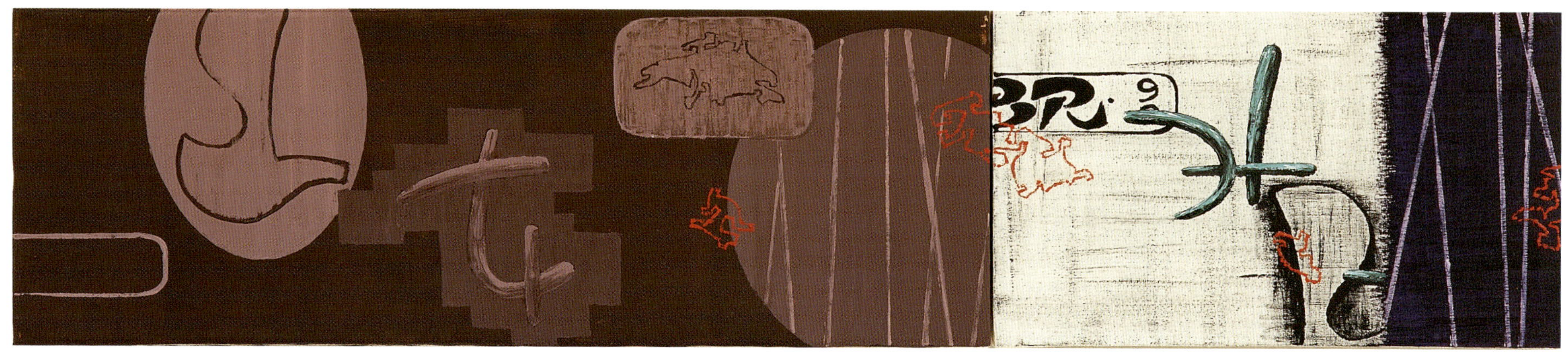
BR. 9

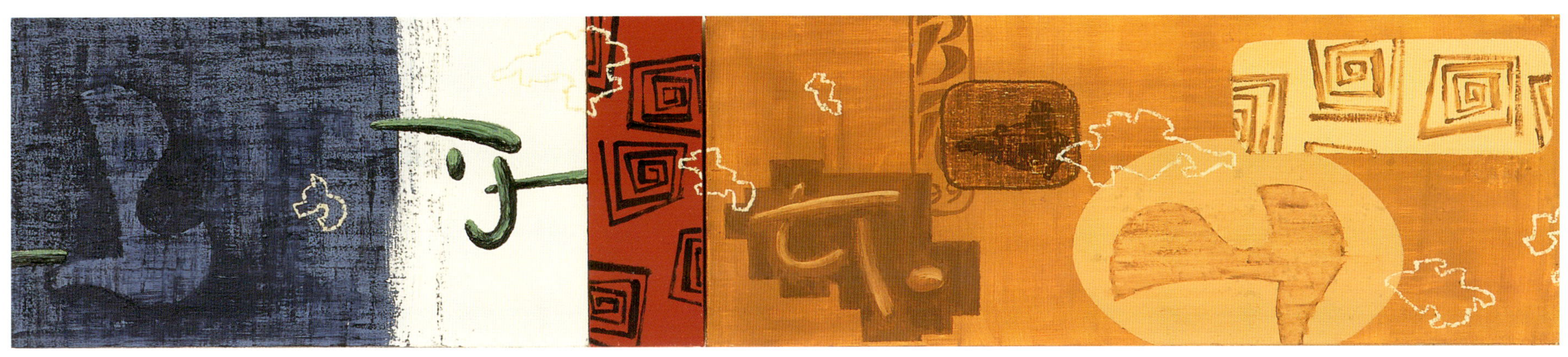

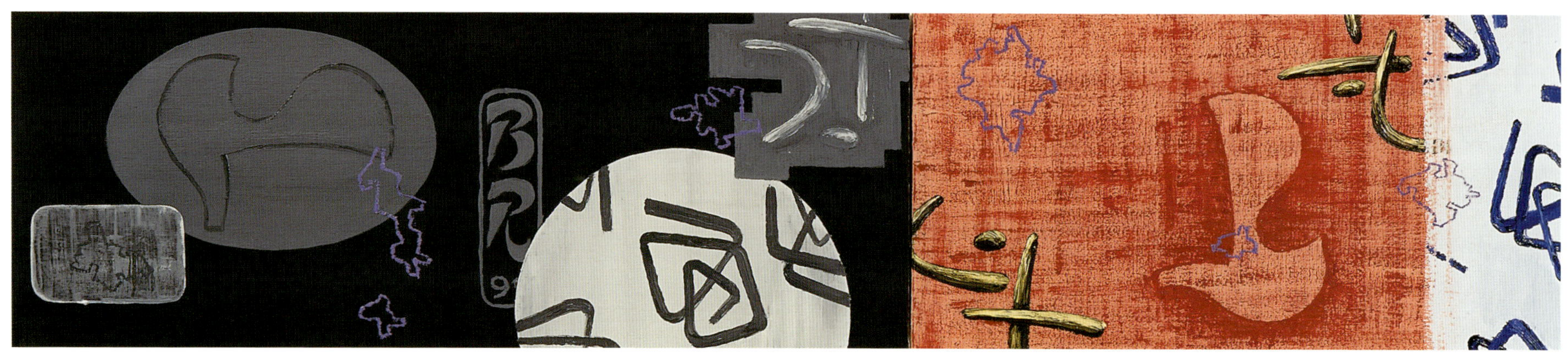

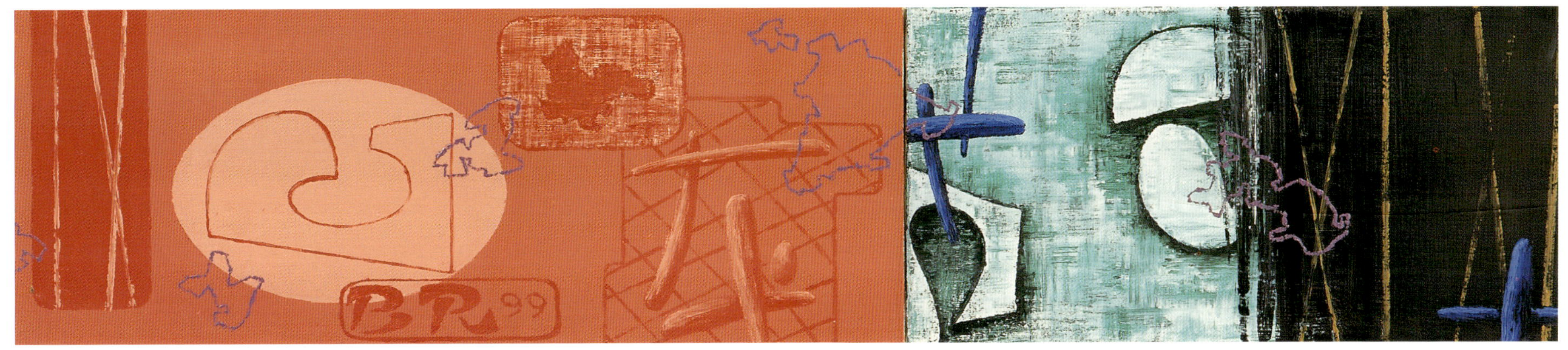

BR 99

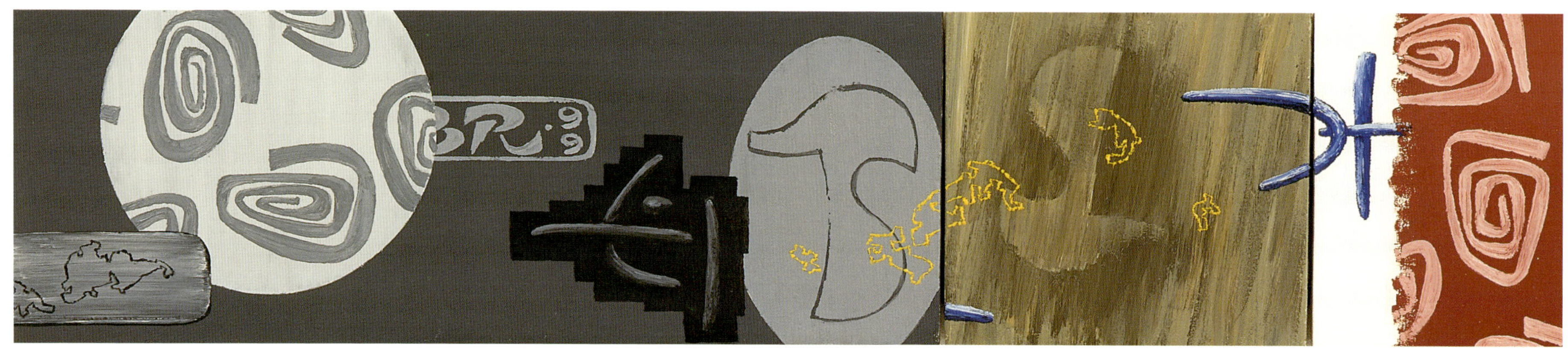

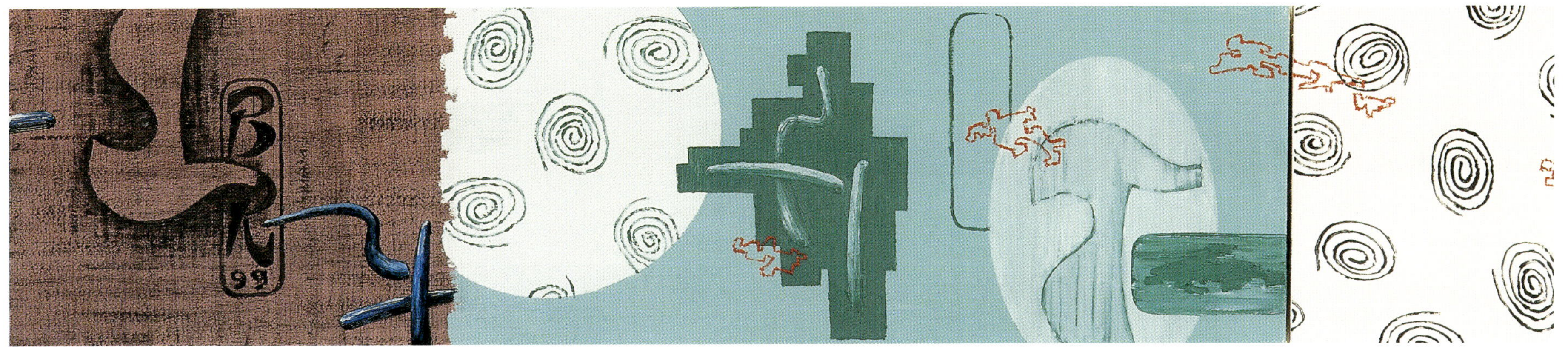

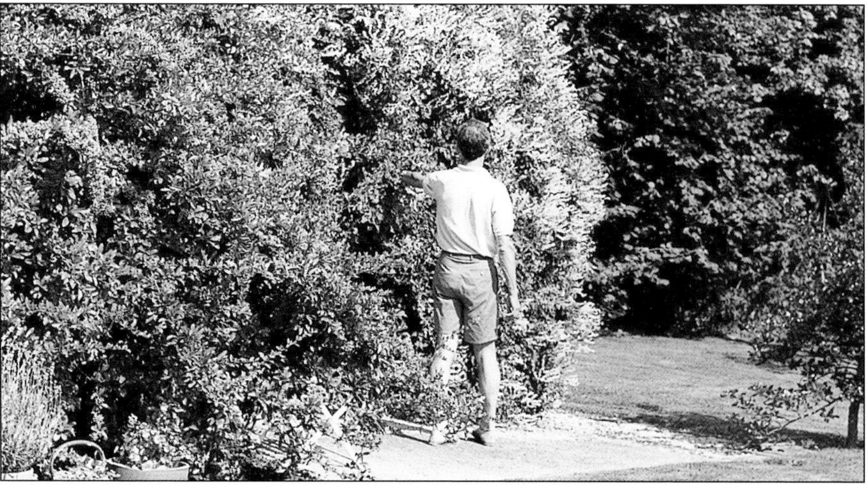

Bruce Russell was born in 1946. He studied at Chelsea School of Art before becoming one of the first Cheltenham Fellows. He has taught widely, including St Martins and Newcastle, where he opened the University Gallery. He is currently Professor of Fine Art and Director of the Stanley Picker Gallery at Kingston University. Bruce Russell has been represented in many national and international exhibitions over the past 30 years and has work in private an public collections across the world.

List of Works (all oil on canvas)

1.	GMT#3 RASHOMON	1998	12X55"		15.	GMT#26 TEN MINUTE TARE	1999	12X55"
2.	SALMAGUNDI#24	1997	12X40"		16.	GMT#22 I REMEMBER FABLON	1999	12X55"
3.	SALMAGUNDI#22	1997	12X40"		17.	GMT#33 SULTAN'S SLIPPER	1999	12X55"
4.	RIFT	1980	65X78"		18.	GMT#39 LAST TRAIN TO SAN FERNANDO	1999	12X55"
5.	PENUMBRA	1989	96X96"					
6.	LUNDY, BISCAY	1984	84X72"		19.	GMT#38 PARIS PULLMAN	1999	12X55"
7.	MASTABA	1989	66X78"		20.	GMT#21 MODERN MODES	1999	12X55"
8.	GALLOWGATE#15	1977	78X78"		21.	GMT#36 CUBAN HEEL	1999	12X55"
9.	OCCLUDED FRONT	1990	78X90"		22.	GMT#25 EVENINGS AT THE REGAL	1999	12X55"
10.	AILSA	1985	78X66"		23.	GMT#40 EEL PIE ISLAND	1999	12X55"
11.	SALMAGUNDI#3	1997	18X24"		24.	GMT#29 SKYLON NIGHTS	1999	12X55"
12.	GMT#2 THE SEVEN SAMURAI	1998	12X55"		25.	GMT#28 KEY BISCAYNE	1999	12X55"
13.	GMT#24 ZABRISKE POINT	1999	12X55"		26.	GMT#31 TOM HARK	1999	12X55"
14.	GMT#30 TURKISH DELIGHT	1999	12X55"		27.	GMT#32 CHELSEA CLASSIC	1999	12X55"

Photo Credits

Vince Wade: 4, 5, 23, 24, 28, 29, 30, 31, 32, 33, 36, 37, 38, 39, 40, 41, 42, 43, 44, 45

Alison Russell: 1, 2, 3, 26, 27, 34, 46

Prudence Cuming Associates: 7, 10, 11, 14, 18, 20, 23

Cover: Eel Pie Island 1999 (detail)

Cover photograhpy: Vince Wade

Published and distributed by Art Books International in collaboration with Kingston University.

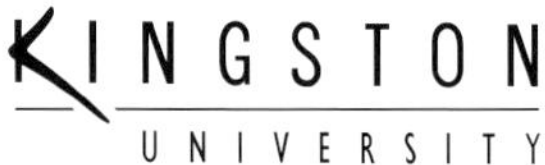

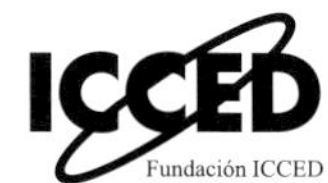

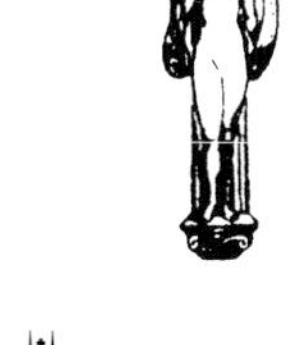

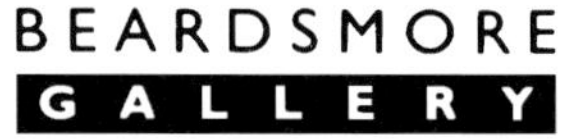

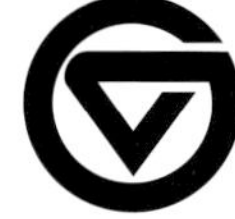

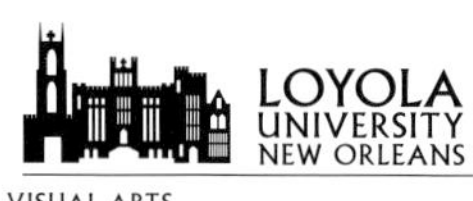

Art Books International

1 Stewart's Court, 220 Stewart's Road, London SW8 4UD

Glyphs, Morphs and Tropes is an original Beardsmore Gallery exhibition: October 7th - 31st 1999 (Tuesday - Saturday 10am - 5pm, and by appointment

The show will travel to Escuela Nacional de Bellas Artes, Buenos Aires, Argentina; ICCED, San Luis Argentina; Loyola University, New Orleans, USA; GVSU, Michigan, USA through 2000

Designed by David Wood

Typeface: Eurostile Extended

Printed by Butler and Tanner.

A catalogue record for this book is available in the British Library

ISBN 1-89999-09-4